This book is dedicated to the avenger of the blood of Hussein, the Awaited Savior, may God hasten his blessed return.

@2023 Sayed Mahdi Modarresi
All Rights Reserved
Enlight Press
Social Media: @SayedModarresi

عَنِ الرَّيَّانِ بْنِ شَبِيبٍ، عَنِ الرِّضَا (عليه السّلام) أَنَّهُ قَالَ: "يَا ابْنَ شَبِيبٍ: إِنْ كُنْتَ بَاكِياً لِشَيْءٍ فَابْكِ لِلْحُسَيْنِ بْنِ عَلِيٍّ (عليه السّلام)، فَإِنَّهُ ذُبِحَ كَمَا يُذْبَحُ الْكَبْشُ، وَقُتِلَ مَعَهُ مِنْ أَهْلِ بَيْتِهِ ثَمَانِيَةَ عَشَرَ رَجُلًا مَا لَهُمْ فِي الْأَرْضِ شَبِيهُونَ، وَلَقَدْ بَكَتِ السَّمَاوَاتُ السَّبْعُ وَالْأَرَضُونَ لِقَتْلِهِ. يَا ابْنَ شَبِيبٍ: إِنْ بَكَيْتَ عَلَى الْحُسَيْنِ (عليه السّلام) حَتَّى تَصِيرَ دُمُوعُكَ عَلَى خَدَّيْكَ غَفَرَ اللَّهُ لَكَ كُلَّ ذَنْبٍ أَذْنَبْتَهُ، صَغِيراً كَانَ أَوْ كَبِيراً، قَلِيلًا كَانَ أَوْ كَثِيراً. يَا ابْنَ شَبِيبٍ: إِنْ سَرَّكَ أَنْ تَلْقَى اللَّهَ عَزَّ وَ جَلَّ وَ لَا ذَنْبَ عَلَيْكَ فَزُرِ الْحُسَيْنَ (عليه السّلام). يَا ابْنَ شَبِيبٍ: إِنْ سَرَّكَ أَنْ تَسْكُنَ الْغُرَفَ الْمَبْنِيَّةَ فِي الْجَنَّةِ مَعَ النَّبِيِّ وَ آلِهِ صَلَّى اللَّهُ عَلَيْهِمْ فَالْعَنْ قَتَلَةَ الْحُسَيْنِ. يَا ابْنَ شَبِيبٍ: إِنْ سَرَّكَ أَنْ يَكُونَ لَكَ مِنَ الثَّوَابِ مِثْلُ مَا لِمَنِ اسْتُشْهِدَ مَعَ الْحُسَيْنِ فَقُلْ مَتَى مَا ذَكَرْتَهُ: يَا لَيْتَنِي كُنْتُ مَعَهُمْ فَأَفُوزَ فَوْزاً عَظِيماً.

Rayyan ibn Shabeeb, narrated that Imam Ali ar-Rida (peace be upon him), said to him:
"O' son of Shabeeb, if you weep for anything, weep for Hussein ibn Ali (peace be upon him), for he was slaughtered like a lamb. Eighteen members of his household were killed with him, none of whom had any equal on earth. The seven heavens and the earth wept for his killing. O' son of Shabeeb, if you weep for Hussein (peace be upon him) until your tears flow down your cheeks, Allah will forgive every sin you have committed, whether small or great, whether few or many. O' son of Shabeeb, if it pleases you to meet Allah, exalted and glorified, without any sin upon you, then visit Hussein (peace be upon him). O' son of Shabeeb, if it pleases you to dwell in the upper chambers of Paradise with the Prophet and his family, may Allah bless them, then curse the killers of Hussein. O' son of Shabeeb, if it pleases you to have a reward like that of those who were martyred with Hussein, then say whenever you mention them: 'O', I wish I had been with them so that I would have achieved a great victory.'"

CONTENTS

INTRODUCTION	7
ABOUT THIS BOOK	19
THE EVE OF ASHURA	25
THE DAY OF ASHURA	29
THE COMPANIONS	33
MEMBERS OF HUSSEIN'S FAMILY	47
ALI AL-AKBAR	48
THE SONS OF LADY ZEINAB	51
QASSEM, SON OF HASSAN	52
ABBAS IBN ALI	55
THE INFANT	60
IMAM HUSSEIN	63
THE CATASTOPHE	73
THE IMMEDIATE AFTERMATH	75

INTRODUCTION

Fourteen centuries ago, on Ashura, the tenth day of the new Islamic year, in the early afternoon, on a sand dune in Karbala, south of the present-day Iraqi capital, a convoy of men, women, and children met a brutal massacre at the hands of an army numbering over thirty thousand. Though mythically defiant, the small camp had little chance of survival, as it was deprived from water and food in the scorching desert. Consequently, the monstrous military force swiftly and completely annihilated them within a few hours. All the men, along with a dozen children and infants, were slaughtered, while the remaining women and children were taken captive. The caravan, along with the severed heads of the martyrs, was paraded throughout the nation in a degrading spectacle amid deranged festivities and celebrations, until finally, everything came to an end. Everything.

Today, Ashura brings more than 1.5 billion people worldwide to a standstill. This solemn commemoration of the most tragic event is observed as a public holiday from India to Egypt, from Azerbaijan to Yemen, and in communities across every province and capital around the globe. The significance of Ashura is immortalized through grand re-enactments and heartfelt lamentations on a mass scale. Even in Europe and North America, millions gather to observe Ashura, participating in processions that showcase a profound outpouring of emotion. Despite over a millennium passing since the event, the pain remains unhealed, and its inspiring message continues to resonate. To a quarter of the world's population, it is a legend of such immense power that it transcends ordinary bounds. Ashura truly becomes larger than life.

The tragedy of Ashura stands as the pinnacle of the most sorrowful events. It is a meta-historical tragedy, reaching a cataclysmic magnitude that defies comprehension. Its profound impact is enough to make even the most hardened hearts bleed, as it unveils the unimaginable savagery unleashed by those who resemble beasts despite possessing human form.

Below is a very short summary of events that led up to the tragedy in Karbala, culminating in the martyrdom of the hero at the center of the legend; Imam Hussein.

For twenty-five tumultuous years following the death of the Prophet, his nation experienced a state of utter disarray. Despite its vast expanse spanning from Africa to the distant corners of the once-mighty Persian Empire, and its status as a formidable military and economic power, the nation teetered on the brink of implosion. fleeting period of just governance under the rule of Imam Ali, the Prophet's esteemed confidante and the sole appointed successor. Although he had endured a period of effective house arrest during the preceding caliphate, Imam Ali seized the opportunity to restore stability and righteousness.

Subversive actions and wars relentlessly targeted Imam Ali, persisting until his untimely and brutal assassination while in prayer at the mosque of Kufa. Simultaneously, his longstanding adversary and mastermind of his heinous assassination, Mu'awiyah, son of Abu Sufyan, craftily employed Machiavellian tactics to usurp control of the Muslim empire. With cunning maneuvering, Mu'awiyah overthrew Imam Hassan, Hussein's elder brother, who had assumed leadership after their father's demise.

Under the shadow of Mu'awyah's brutality and deception, Hassan found himself compelled to accept the terms of this settlement. Among its provisions, it stipulated that governance would be returned to Imam Hassan after Mu'awyah's demise, or in the event of Hassan's passing, the mantle would fall to his brother, Hussein. However, once he had secured his position and solidified his grip on power, Mu'awyah moved to annul this agreement. Rather than handing over authority to Hussein upon his death, Mu'awyah forcefully enthroned his bastard son Yazeed, and took the pledge of allegiance for him while he was still alive. By using promises and ultimatums, using carrots as well as sticks, tribal leaders were properly incentivized to take him as heir to the throne.

After twenty two years of mob rule, much bloodshed, and widespread oppression, Mu'awyah died and power was transferred to Yazeed, in contravention of the treaty. A corrupt, sexually degenerate, sadistic hedonist, Yazeed was known by all as the poster child of savagery and moral depravity.

Hussein, the son of Imam Ali, stood as the sole surviving grandson of the Prophet, carrying within him the noble lineage of a long line of divinely appointed Messengers. In every aspect, he bore a striking resemblance to his revered grandfather, endearing him to the hearts of Muslims who held him in utmost reverence for his impeccable character and righteous demeanor.

People had long tasted the bitterness of oppression under Mu'awyah and were fully aware of what the nation under his illegitimate son would mean. So they turned to Hussein, not just because he was the grandson of their prophet, the son of their martyred leader, and the rightful ruler, but because he was supremely pious, generous, and knowledgeable; the one who best preserved the ideals and values of Islam. In addition to all of this, he was, in the eyes of the faithful, a Godly saint.

Before long, Hussein was inundated with a deluge of letters pleading with him to come to Kufa, his father's former administrative capital. In their correspondence, Kufans implored him "in God's name" to come to them and assume the reigns of power. Sensing that he bore a responsibility to uphold justice and prevent oppression, to promote goodness and provide guidance, Hussein rose to the occasion. This had been the mission of prophets before him, and now he felt as though its weight had fallen upon his shoulders and their banner was now in his hand. So he responded to the peoples' call, not out of aspiration for power or desire for worldly vanities. Such things were far removed from the character of the Prophet's closest family members who strived for the sake of the hereafter rather than the sake of this world; but to spread justice and repel tyranny.

Hussein dispatched his cousin and closest confidante, Muslim b. Aqeel, to Kufa. His mission was to assess the situation and provide council on whether the calls for Hussein to move to Kufa were genuine. He replied to their letters, saying that if their treatment of his cousin shows them to be truthful in their entreaties and ready to assist him in his mission, then he will make the journey to them.

From his own side, Yazeed sent letters to the various provinces of the Muslim empire, demanding that the governors submit to his rule and demand the pledge of allegiance from the people; he ordered them to execute whoever refused, specifically mentioning Hussein b. Ali for two reasons:

1. In the depths of his soul, Yazeed knew that he had usurped the rightful place of Hussein and the position that was lawfully his from a number of angles; the least of which was the treaty signed between his father and Imam Hassan, the terms of which meant that Yazeed's government faced a detrimental crisis of legitimacy.

2. People loved Imam Hussein because of the qualities, merits and knowledge possessed, as well as his family, who were moral icons. The people also desired him as a ruler because they saw him as sincere and had every inclination towards justice and righteousness.

Registering his official rejection of Yazeed's regime, Hussein refused to pledge allegiance to Yazeed on conscientious grounds, saying that he had done so because of his infamous wickedness, violent temperament, and established vile demeanor. Knowing full well that Hussein is the biggest impediment to his rule, Yazeed ordered his governor in Medina to force Hussein into acquiescence, or sever his head!

After a tense interaction with the governor, in which Hussein spurned allegiance to Yazeed, he was threatened with execution. Subsequently, Hussein, his family, and a small band of supporters left their sanctuary in Medina and headed for Mecca in the pitch black darkness. Whilst there, Hussein received thousands more letters pleading with him to come to Kufa and lead a revolt against the tyrannical regime. Meanwhile, he dispatched his cousin and close confidant Muslim ibn Aqeel to Kufa, where eighteen thousand people willingly offered their pledge of allegiance to him as Hussein's special envoy. Encouraged by these developments, Muslim sent word to the Imam that many had vowed to stand with him against Yazeed and pledged their oath to Imam Hussein.

Hussein made it clear in various sermons that he was not interested in civil war, nor was he seeking an adventure in self-interest. His only objective was to preserve the integrity of the faith and its values. Having made his position clear, Hussein set out for Kufa with most members of his extended household and a number of loyal men and women. But the situation quickly turned against him, as the authorities moved to quell popular dissent in Kufa. Muslim ibn Aqeel was apprehended after a violent skirmish. While Hussein was still en route, Muslim was brutally executed and thrown off the roof of a building housing the governor Ubaullah ibn Zyad.

The government mobilized more than thirty thousand troops, led by Omar ibn Sa'd, against Hussein and the two sides met in an area known as Karbala. With Hussein's steadfast refusal to submit to the tyranny of Yazeed, his path was intercepted by an army which also cut off access to water and besieged them in the desolate desert. Fully conscious of the looming massacre, Hussein earnestly asked his companions to leave him and save themselves. His disciples, made up of the elderly and the young, the rich and the poor, those of noble lineage as well as slaves and peasants. Even a Christian family joined him, all vowing to defend him and his family to the last breath. "May the wild beasts eat us alive if we ever abandoned you" one said. "I would rather be killed, burnt, and have my ashes dispersed in the air, and have that done a thousand times, before I leave you and your family" said another. They were resolute. So much so, that Hussein declared "I do not know of any companions more loyal than my own".

With no food, water, or a means to reaching safe haven, the camp of Hussein was ambushed; on the tenth day of Muharram, fifty one years after the Prophet Mohammad's passing, his grandson Hussein and his small band of followers faced a force more than five-hundred times larger than their own.

The enemy's assault was so vicious, wild beasts would be put to shame. Hussein's valiant companions fought with unyielding determination, displaying unwavering loyalty, unparalleled courage, and resolute conviction. Every noble quality found its embodiment within them.

It was a battle etched in the annals of legend, unlike any other, as the companions of Hussein fought heroically, and selflessly offered their lives in sacrifice for their revered leader. In a chilling display of brutality, thirst-stricken women and innocent children were mercilessly slain. Yazeed's bloodthirsty mercenaries spared no mercy, claiming the lives of the majority of Hussein's cousins, siblings, and even his own beloved children. Their heinous acts stained the pages of history with unfathomable cruelty.

His six month old infant. The child was about to die of dehydration. In a final desperate plea, Hussein beseeched his adversaries, "You have slain my friends and family, leaving me with no one but this helpless child. His mother's milk has run dry, so grant him a sip of water." In an unprecedented turn, the enemy ranks found themselves divided. Some questioned, "If men are deemed criminals, what wrong has befallen this innocent child to deserve death?"

Recognizing the potential for dissent within his own forces, the enemy commander issued an unthinkable order. A three-pronged arrow, tipped with poison, was released, severing the infant's head from jugular vein to jugular vein, while his anguished father watched him whither away.

Having committed the most heinous of crimes, the homicidal savages would not be deterred from anything else. Hussein had borne witness to the merciless slaughter of his beloved family, endured excruciating torment for three agonizing days, wounded from countless stabs. He became an altar upon which converged thousands of swords, spears, knives, and rocks. While reminding them that he was their Prophet's own son, Hussein was sadistically butchered, while they cheered and whistled in mad hysteria.

The heartrending tragedy continued, with the severing of the blessed heads - including those of the children - and were raised on pikes. The grief-stricken family of the Prophet were taken captive and sent to Yazeed. They were subjected to a degrading spectacle as they were paraded along a 700km route, enduring the lash of whips and unspeakable torment.

Amidst this atmosphere of chaos and brutality, the martyrdom of Hussein and his companions elevated them into the quintessential paragons of virtue, faith, purity, generosity, and bravery. Meanwhile, their adversaries became symbolic of every evil, falsehood, and vice.

Hussein is seen as a man who faced death, so that humanity understands the meaning of life. He was slain once, yet his spirit persists, resurrected countless times. Although he fell in isolation, bereft of allies, millions now march annually to answer his call. He was parched, but is remembered whenever we quench our thirst. Despite enduring profound hatred, he emerged as the embodiment of compassion, his light transformed into an eternal flame that ignites the hearts of seekers. Though he perished in hunger, his name nourishes hundreds of millions. His tents were desecrated and set ablaze, but his name adorns homes in every corner of the world.

Hussein became a singular figure who fills history with his grace and grandeur, becoming a meta-historical legend, epitomizing the perennial struggle between good and evil.

ABOUT THIS BOOK

This book presents a concise retelling of events that transpired on the day of Ashura. While it is an authentic passion narrative, many details have been intentionally omitted for the sake of brevity.

A vast array of literature, comprising tens of thousands of books, exists on this subject, offering readers the opportunity to delve into more extensive explorations.

What sets this book apart are a few notable attributes:

This book has been crafted using simple English language, making it accessible to a wide range of readers. To maintain the authenticity and provide additional depth, certain highlights and epic moments are quoted in their original language as side-notes. This enables readers to immerse themselves in both versions, should they desire to do so.

Moreover, all the epic tales and poems included in this book have been translated into verse. This approach aims to preserve the poetic essence of the original language while staying faithful to the intended meaning. The endeavor has been to capture the rhythmic beauty and emotional resonance of the verses, enhancing the overall reading experience

Furthermore, this book draws upon a foundation of mainstream and reputable sources for its content. These sources include influential works such as Tarikh al-Tabari by Muhammad ibn Jarir al-Tabari (d. 923 CE), Al-Lohoof by Sayyed ibn Tawus (d. 1266 CE), Kamil al-Ziyarat by Jafar ibn Qulawayh al-Qommi (d. 978 CE), Kitab al-Irshad by Shaykh al-Mufid (d. 1022 CE), Maqtal al-Husayn by al-Khwarizmi (d. 1171 CE), Bihar al-Anwār by Allamah al-Majlisi (d. 1699 CE).

In addition to these historical texts, it incorporates insights from contemporary compilations like Nafasul Mahmoom by Shaykh Abbas al-Qommi (d. 1941 CE).

Nafasul Mahmoom deserves particular mention, as it meticulously draws upon a diverse range of reliable sources. The author, leveraging expertise in the science of Hadith and historical references, presents a comprehensive depiction of the events. By incorporating these respected and trusted sources, the book strives to provide a well-rounded and accurate account.

I pray that this book helps acquaint more

people with the saga of Ashura and the agonizing tale of Imam Hussein's martyrdom.

Sayed Mahdi al-Modarresi
Holy City of Karbala

8th of Dhul Hijjah, 1444 AH
(The day of Imam Hussein's departure from Makkah towards Karbala)

Imam al-Redha has said[1],

"Verily, the day of Hussein's martyrdom has bruised our eyelids and poured our tears. It has humiliated our noble ones with affliction and adversity and inherited us sorrow and calamity until the Day of Judgement. So let the weepers weep for the likes Hussein, for weeping over him erases great sins."

Imam al-Mahdi states,

[1] «إِنَّ يَوْمَ الْحُسَيْنِ أَقْرَحَ جُفُونَنَا، وَأَسْبَلَ دُمُوعَنَا، وَأَذَلَّ عَزِيزَنَا بِأَرْضِ كَرْبٍ وَبَلَاءٍ، أَوْرَثَتْنَا الْكَرْبَ وَالْبَلَاءَ إِلَى يَوْمِ الِانْقِضَاءِ. فَعَلَى مِثْلِ الْحُسَيْنِ فَلْيَبْكِ الْبَاكُونَ، فَإِنَّ الْبُكَاءَ عَلَيْهِ يَحُطُّ الذُّنُوبَ الْعِظَامَ»

السَّلَامُ عَلَى مَنْ نُكِثَتْ ذِمَّتُهُ، السَّلَامُ عَلَى مَنْ هُتِكَتْ حُرْمَتُهُ، السَّلَامُ عَلَى مَنْ أُرِيقَ بِالظُّلْمِ دَمُهُ، السَّلَامُ عَلَى الْمُغَسَّلِ بِدَمِ الْجِرَاحِ، السَّلَامُ عَلَى الْمُجَرَّعِ بِكَأْسَاتِ الرِّمَاحِ، السَّلَامُ عَلَى الْمُضَامِ الْمُسْتَبَاحِ، السَّلَامُ عَلَى الْمَهْجُورِ فِي الْوَرَى، السَّلَامُ عَلَى مَنْ تَوَلَّى دَفْنَهُ أَهْلُ الْقُرَى، السَّلَامُ عَلَى الْمَقْطُوعِ الْوَتِينِ، السَّلَامُ عَلَى الْمُحَامِي بِلَا مُعِينٍ. السَّلَامُ عَلَى الشَّيْبِ الْخَضِيبِ، السَّلَامُ عَلَى الْخَدِّ التَّرِيبِ، السَّلَامُ عَلَى الْبَدَنِ السَّلِيبِ، السَّلَامُ عَلَى الثَّغْرِ الْمَقْرُوعِ بِالْقَضِيبِ، السَّلَامُ عَلَى الْوَدَجِ الْمَقْطُوعِ، السَّلَامُ عَلَى الرَّأْسِ الْمَرْفُوعِ، السَّلَامُ عَلَى الْأَجْسَامِ الْعَارِيَةِ فِي الْفَلَوَاتِ، تَنْهَشُهَا الذِّئَابُ الْعَادِيَاتُ، وَ تَخْتَلِفُ إِلَيْهَا السِّبَاعُ الضَّارِيَاتُ..[2]

[2] Zyarat al-Nahyah, Al-Mazar al-Kabeer, Al-Mashhadani

Salam to the one surrounded by mobs,
Salam to the public slaughter, heart throbs
Salam to the bereaved and patient one,
Salam to the oppressed, no helper to be won.
Salam to the violated rights and dignity,
Salam to the desecrated sanctity.
Salam to the unjustly shed blood,

Salam to wounds, where crimson floods.
Salam to the stranger left on the ground,
Salam to the defender, no savior found.
Salam to the blood-dyed, solemn beard,
Salam to the cheek, with dust adhered.
Salam to the dusty cheek, burdened with strife,
Salam to the butchered body, stolen from life.
Salam to the front teeth, met with a rod's might
Salam to the head, raised high, a tragic sight.

THE EVE OF ASHURA

Imam Ali ibn al-Hussein recounted the scene that unfolded at dusk, "Imam Hussein gathered his companions. After praising God, he said, 'I do not know of companions more loyal or better than my companions. Nor a family more obedient or committed to keeping their kinship than my family.' He then said, 'I have absolved you of your oath of allegiance. Seize the cover of darkness and escape. These people only want me and if they kill me they won't go after you.'"

With incredible fidelity, every companion and family member rose to express their steadfast pledge to stand by his side and defend him until the end.

Hussein then addressed them, saying, "you will all be killed tomorrow and none will be spared." They replied in unison, "praise be to God for honoring us with dying for your sake." So Imam Hussein prayed for them and instructed them to gather the tents closer together, forming a protective circle around the women and children. To further fortify their defenses, Imam Hussein told his companions to dig a moat behind the camp to hinder any potential attack from the rear. The moat was then filled with wood and hay, then set ablaze, presenting a formidable obstacle for the enemy.

The Imam and his companions stood in prayer and supplication until dawn. It has been reported that during the night, thirty two of the soldiers of Omar ibn Sa'd also joined Hussein's camp.

Imam Ali ibn al-Hussein - who was extremely ill - says: "that night, my aunt Zeinab was attending to me. Suddenly, she overheard Imam Hussein speaking in the tent of John, who was sharpening the swords. The Imam said, "O' Dunya! Woe unto you for you are a terrible friend. Day and night, you have killed many who sought you. Every living thing will follow this path, for how near is the point of departure. I leave matters in the hands of the Majestic Lord." Imam al-Sajjad said, "I knew what my father was saying and despite choking up with tears, I remained silent. But my aunt Zeinab couldn't suppress her grief and went to my father's tent wailing, and saying[1], 'I wish death would end my life.. O' successor of those that have passed, and protector of those that have remained. today my mother Fatima has died, and my father Ali and my brother Hassan..' So my father comforted her and

---

1 «وا ثكلاه! ليت الموت أعدمني الحياة، اليوم ماتت أمي فاطمة، وأبي علي وأخي الحسن..».

brought her back to my tent."

At sunrise, my father fell asleep briefly. When he woke up, he said, "I saw God's Messenger and he told me, 'my son! You are the martyr of the family of Mohammad and tonight you shall be my guest. Hurry up, for indeed the time has come to migrate from this world.'

THE DAY OF ASHURA

As the tenth of Muharram dawned, Hussein, the grandson of the Messenger of Allah, led his followers for the morning Prayer. Adorned in his grandfather's armor and turban, and wielding his father's sword, he stood before his companions and commenced his address. He praised Allah and His Prophet, then said[1], "Allah has willed that you and I shall be killed on this day. So embrace patience and engage in battle."

Hussein then asked for his horse. He mounted the noble steed and began preparing his companions for battle. He appointed Habib ibn Mudhaher as commander of the right flank, Muslim ibn Awsajah leader of the left flank, and his brother Abbas at the center, as the flag bearer. The Imam asked those in the center to stand firm, so they surrounded him like a ring.[2]

The forces of Omar ibn Sa'd began to encircle the camp of Hussein. Shimr attempted to approach from behind, but was met with the

1 »إن الله تعالى قد أذن في قتلي وقتلكم في هذا اليوم فعليكم بالصبر والقتال«

2 قال الحسين لأصحاب القلب: »أثبتوا«. وأحاطوا بالحسين من كل جانب حتى جعلوه في مثل الحلقة

fiery moat, which blocked his path. Furious, he shouted "O' Hussein, you have hastened towards the hellfire!" Hussein replied, "Woe unto you! You are more deserving of the hellfire." In response, Muslim ibn Awsajah sought to launch an arrow in Shimr's direction, but Hussein intervened, proclaiming, "I detest being the one to ignite war with them."

Hussein then mounted a camel so as to rise higher and allow people to see and hear him clearly. He praised God and sent blessings upon the angels and prophets. He then introduced himself and reminded them of the letters they had sent to him in which they invited him to come to Kufa. He warned them of disobeying God and of waging war against the Prophet's progeny and counseled them against evil.

Hussein's loyal companions, like Habib ibn Mudhaher and Zuhair ibn al-Qayn, stepped forward to deliver impassioned speeches, but the enemy did not heed their advice and, instead praised Ibn Zyad and hurled profanities at them.

Enemy troops brazenly issued an ultimatum, "either you and your companions pay allegiance to Yazid, or we shall kill you all right here".

The Imam dismounted his camel and returned to form his troops.

A letter had reached Omar ibn Sa'd from

Ibn Zyad, bearing an ominous command. Hussein's access to water must be obstructed at all costs, without a single drop to quench his thirst. Amr ibn al-Hajjaj swiftly led five hundred horsemen to fortify the riverbank. Abdullah ibn al-Ḥoṣayn al-Azdi addressed Hussein, saying "Behold the water before us, resembling the blue sky above. By God, you shall not taste a single sip until thirst claims you and your companions!"[1]

Omar ibn Sa'd and his troops men drew nearer to the camp of Hussein. Omar took a bow and shot an arrow in the direction of the Imam, saying, "Bear witness for me with the ruler that I was the first to shoot!"[2] The arrows then followed like rain, causing many injuries among Hussein's men. The Imam called upon his followers:

"Rise to the inevitable death. May God bestow His mercy upon you. These arrows are the messengers of these people to you."[3] The battle was engulfed and after a short time, a number of Hussein's companions were seen slain on the sands.

Imam Ali ibn al-Hussein has said, "the harder it became for Imam Hussein, the brighter his face would shine. His composure would deepen, and his heart would find serenity. His devoted companions would marvel at his unwavering laughter in the face of death, for he knew no fear. Addressing his loyal followers, the Imam would impart words

1 نادى أحد أوباش اهل الكوفة: «يا حسين، ألا تنظر إلى الماء كأنه كبد السماء، والله لا تذوقون منه قطرة واحدة حتى تموتوا عطشاً!» فقال الحسين عليه السلام: «اللهم أقتله عطشاً ولا تغفر له أبداً». وروى من رآه بعد معركة كربلاء، فقال إنه رآه يشرب الماء حتى يبغر (أي يفيض من فمه) ثم يقيئه، ويصيح: «العطش العطش!»، ثم فيعود فيشرب الماء حتى يبغر ثم يقيئه ويتلظى عطشاً، فما زال ذلك دأبه حتى لفظ نفسه

2 «اشهدوا لي عند الأمير أني أول من رمى! وأقبلت السهام من القوم كأنها المطر!»

3 «قوموا رحمكم الله إلى الموت الذي لا بد منه. هذه السهام رسل القوم إليكم»

of patience and strength, proclaiming, "O' sons of the great ones, be steadfast! Death is but a bridge that transports us from hardship to expansive gardens and eternal bliss. Who among you wouldn't long to be liberated from a prison to a palace? As for our enemies, their fate in death is a transition from opulence to confinement. This was passed down to me by my father, who heard them from the Messenger of God. Surely I have not lied, nor have I been lied to."

THE COMPANIONS

One after the other, Hussein's men then came to their leader and asked for his permission and blessings. They would bid him farewell, saying, "Peace be upon you O' son of God's messenger."[1] The Imam would reply, "We too are not far behind you."[2]

He would then recite the verse, "Among the Believers are men who have been true to their covenant with Allah: of them some have fulfilled their vow, and some of them who still await, and they have not changed in the least."[3]

The companions waged a fierce battle in defense of their leader.

(Below, we will mention a few of their stories)

1 «السلام عليك يابن رسول الله!»

2 «عليك السلام، نحن في الأثر.»

3 «مِنَ الْمُؤْمِنِينَ رِجَالٌ صَدَقُوا مَا عَاهَدُوا اللَّهَ عَلَيْهِ فَمِنْهُمْ مَنْ قَضَى نَحْبَهُ وَمِنْهُمْ مَنْ يَنْتَظِرُ وَمَا بَدَّلُوا تَبْدِيلًا» [23–33]

Hurr al-Ryahi[1]

1 الحر بن يزيد الرياحي رضوان الله عليه

Hurr commanded a legion in the enemy camp and had been sent by the regime to apprehend Hussein. When he saw that the enemy intended to kill Imam Hussein, and heard his pleas for help, he asked Omar ibn Sa'd, "are you really going to fight this man?" Omar replied, "by God, a fight that will see the falling of heads and amputating of hands!"

Hurr began to shake. His companion said, "I have known you among the bravest of men!" Hurr replied, "By Allah, I see myself having to choose between paradise and hell, and I shall never choose anything over paradise, even if I am mutilated and burnt!"

He then slowly began to inch farther from his camp and closer to Hussein. He placed his hand over his head and said, "O' Lord! I am returning to You. I seek your redemption, for I have struck fear and terror into the hearts of the children of your Messenger.." When Hurr reached Hussein, he addressed him, saying, "may I be ransomed for you, O' son of God's messenger. I am the one who blocked the path of return upon you and forced you into this land. I didn't think these people would reject your advice. Will you give me a chance to repent?" Hussein replied, "yes. God Has accepted your penitence."[2]

2 قال الحر: «يابن رَسولِ الله، هَل لي مِن تَوبَة»؟ فقالَ الحسين: «نَعَم، تابَ اللّٰهُ عَلَيكَ»

Hurr said, "since I was the first to come to

war against you, I wish to be the first to die before you."

Hussein gave him permission to go. He returned to admonish the enemy, to no avail. So he fought them valiantly with unmatched courage, and became the first of Hussein's companions to die.

Muslim ibn Awsajah[1]

He was the deputy of Muslim ibn Aqeel in Kufa, in charge of receiving money and buying weapons, as well as securing pledges of support for the Imam. On Ashura, Muslim displayed incredible strength and patience as he fought against the enemy. When the dust settled, Muslim was seen lying on the ground. Imam Hussein came to him when he was about to die. The Imam prayed for him, saying, *"O' Muslim! May Allah have mercy on you."*

Habib ibn Mudhaher approached him, saying, *"your departure pains me. Had I not been joining you shortly, I would love to know if you had any last wishes so I could fulfill them."* In his dying breath, Muslim pointed to Hussein and said[2], *"May Allah bless you. I advise you take care of him. Defend him until you die."* Habib replied, *"By the Lord of the Kaaba I shall do that and make you proud!"* It wasn't long before Habib surrendered his soul before Hussein.

1 مسلم بن عوسجة الأسدي الكوفي رضوان الله عليه، من أصحاب رسول الله ومن أبطال العرب في صدر الاسلام

2 قالَ لَهُ مُسلِمٌ: «فَإِنِّي أُوصِيكَ بِهذا ـ وأشارَ بِيَدِهِ إلى الحُسَينِ عليه السلام ـ فَقاتِل دونَهُ حَتّى تَموتَ». فَقالَ لَهُ حَبيب: «لَأَنعَمَنَّكَ عَينا»

Burair ibn Khudhair[1]

١ بُرَير بن خُضَير الهَمْداني المِشْرَقي رضوان الله عليه، من أشراف الكوفة ومن شيوخ القرّاء

Burair came toward the enemy camp and challenged them to come and fight him. Yazeed ibn Ma'qel came out and said to him, "O' Burair! What do you think of that which God has done with you?" Burair replied, "I swear to God, He has done nothing but good with me and nothing but bad with you." Yazeed said, "you are lying, and you were never a liar before. Do you not remember telling me that Othman was a sinner and that Mu'awyah was a deviant who misguided others, and that the righteous guide and truthful Imam was Ali ibn Abi Taleb?" Burair replied, "I bear witness that this is my creed and my declaration." Yazeed ibn Ma'qel said, "and I bear witness that you are misguided."

Burair said, "do you want us to perform Mubahila; and invoke God's wrath and curses upon the liar, such that the one who is rightful would kill the one who is wrongful?" Yazeed accepted the challenge and came forward to fight Burair. They exchanged two strikes; a light strike hit Burair, while the other came right on top of Yazeed, splitting his skull in half. He tried to pull out the sword from his head, to no avail. Radhi ibn Munqidh came to his aid, and wrestled with Burair for a while, but Burair threw him to the ground and sat on his chest. He screamed for help from his comrades, and a man named Ka'b ibn Jaber came to his rescue. A soldier said to him, "What do you intend to do? This is Burair, the one who used to teach us the Qur'an in the mosque!" Yet Ka'b did not care. He lodged his spear into Burair's back. He then used the spear to throw off Burair to the side, then struck him with his sword repeatedly until he was martyred.

Amr ibn Qaradhah al-Ansari[1]

Amr ibn Qaradhah had a brother in the army of Omar ibn Sa'd, yet he constantly guarded the Imam, hovering around him like a butterfly. He blocked every sword and every arrow shot in the Imam's direction, shielding them with his hands and face. As long as he was alive, no injuries inflicted the Imam. He attacked the enemy while reciting epics in which he reaffirmed his pledge to defend Hussein with all his might.[2]

Amr asked Hussein for permission to face the enemy. Sayed ibn Tawoos describes him as such: "he battled the enemy like one yearning for heavenly reward and exhausting himself in service to the lord of the heavens." He killed scores of enemy troops until his wounds left him lying on the battlefield. When Hussein came to him, he asked the Imam, "have I fulfilled my pledge to you?" The Imam replied, "yes. you will proceed me to paradise. Convey my salams to God's messenger and tell him that I am right behind you."[3]

A ferocious campaign lasted until noon. Hussein's companions, although small in number, were able to resist the enemy's advance. Omar ibn Sa'd saw that attacking from the front was futile, so he commanded his men to attack from all directions. Shimr yelled, "bring me fire so I can burn these tents

1   عمرو بن قرظة الأنصاري

2   قَدْ عَلِمَتْ كَتِيبَةُ الْأنصار
اِنّى سَاحْمى حَوْزَةَ الذِّمارِي
ضَرْبَ غُلامٍ غَيْرَ نَكسٍ شارِي
دُونَ حُسَيْنٍ مُهْجَتى وَدارِي

3   قال ابن قرظة: «أوفيت يا ابن رسول الله؟» قال: «نعم، أنت أمامي في الجنة، فاقرأ رسول الله مني السلام وأعلمه أني في الأثر»

with everyone in them."¹ The women ran out of the tents wailing. Hussein cried out, "O' son of Jawshan! You are calling for fire to burn my family? May God burn you!"²

A reporter embedded into the enemy camp named Hameed ibn Muslim said to Shimr, "what a horrible thing you are doing! Do you wish to commit two evils at once? Why kill the women and children when you know that the king will be pleased if you only kill the men?" Suddenly, Zuhair ibn al-Qayn along with ten other companions attacked him and pushed him away from the camp. When Omar's men saw Shimr being pushed back, they came to his help killing more of Hussein's companions. With every martyr in the camp, the shrinking of the Imam's army became more visible.

1 صاح الشمر: «عَلَيَّ بِالنَّارِ أُحرِقُهُ عَلَى مَنْ فِيهِ»

2 فقال الحسين: «أَنْتَ الدَّاعِي بِالنَّارِ لِتُحْرِقَ عَلَى أَهْلِي؟ أَحْرَقَكَ اللَّهُ بِالنَّارِ»

Habib ibn Mudhaher[1]

When the noon prayer approached, Abu Thumamah[2] addressed Imam Hussein, saying "O' Aba Abdillah! May I be ransomed for you! I see these men getting closer to you and by Allah, you shall not die before I die for you. [But] I wish to perform this last prayer with you, then meet my Creator after that."

Hussein looked up and said, "you have remembered prayers. May Allah count you among those who pray and remember Him."[3] He then said, "ask these people to stop so that we could perform our prayers." Hoṣayn ibn Tamim replied, "your prayers aren't accepted!" Habib ibn Mudhaher responded to him, "your prayers are accepted while prayers of the progeny of the Prophet are not, you drunkard?" Ibn Tamim was enraged, and launched an attack on Habib, who was able to throw him to the ground. Ibn Tamim's people encircled Habib and he fought them bravely until a sword struck his head, leading to his martyrdom. A fight then ensued, with several men claiming to have killed Habib so they could claim honor and a prize for his murder.

Historians have said that Habib's murder "devastated Hussein" and that he repeatedly said, "I ask recompense from God for myself and my defenders and companions."[4]

1 حبيب بن مُظاهر الأسدي، من خواص أصحاب أمير المؤمنين ومن أعظم أنصار الحسين عليهما السلام

2 أبو ثمامة عمرو بن عبد الله بن كعب الصائدي، تابعي من فرسان العرب ووجوه الشيعة، ومن أصحاب الإمام علي، ثم الحسن والحسين. كان خبيراً بالأسلحة، ومن معتمدي مسلم بن عقيل بالكوفة

3 رفع الحسين (عليه السلام) رأسه ثم قال: «ذكرت الصلاة، جعلك الله من المصلين الذاكرين»

4

41

'Abis ibn Abi Shabeeb[1]

'Abis had vowed to defend Imam Hussein to the end[2]. When he joined the Imam in Karbala his slave Shawdab joined him. 'Abis told Shawdab, "what's on your mind and what will you do?" Shawdab replied, "what else will I do? I shall fight next to the Prophet's grandson until I am killed!" 'Abis said, "that's what I thought you would do. Go to Hussein so that you will be counted among his companions. If I had anyone closer to me than you, I would have sent him to battle before me so that I would grieve for him and be rewarded for my grief." Shawdab went to the Imam, paid his respects, then headed to battle and reached martyrdom.

'Abis then came to the Imam and said, "I swear to Allah, there is no one on earth, close or far from me, who is dearer or more beloved to me than you. And if I could repel death from you with something dearer than my soul, I would I have done so. Peace be upon you O' Aba Abdillah! I take God as my witness that I shall walk in your and your father's footsteps." He then raised his sword and walked towards the enemy, despite having a wound on his forehead.

Rabee' ibn Tameem says, "I had never seen anyone more courageous than 'Abis. So I warned my comrades, 'this black lion is the son of Abi Shabeeb, so do not accept his challenge to fight." 'Abis kept shouting, "is there no man among you?" Omar ibn Sa'd said, "pelt him with stones from all directions." When 'Abis saw his cries falling on deaf ears, he took off his armor and ripped his shirt and charged towards them.

Rabee' says, "I swear to God that I saw two hundred men surrounding him. When they killed him and severed his head, several men claimed they had killed 'Abis!" As they argued, they came to Omar ibn Sa'd. He said, "no single man killed 'Abis".

Abu al-Sha'thaa

Yazeed ibn Zyad, known as Abu al-Sha'thaa, was a master archer. He sat on his knee and shot a hundred arrows. Every time he shot an arrow, the Imam prayed for him, saying[1], *"O' Allah, make his aim accurate and grant him the reward of Paradise.."* All but five arrows hit their targets.

When his arrows were depleted, he got up and said, "only five of my arrows fell to the ground and did not kill their targets. I shall go and kill those five with my sword." He was among the first to be martyred in battle.

His epic was:

"My Lord, I am a supporter of Hussein,

I have abandoned and distanced myself from Ibn Sa'd."[2]

1. «اللهم سدد رميته واجعل ثوابه الجنة»

2. «يا ربي إني للحسين ناصر، ولابن سعد تارك وهاجر»

Aslam, the Turkish Slave

A Turkish slave named Aslam who was bought by Imam Hussein accompanied him from Medina. When the war broke out on the day of Ashura, Aslam sought permission to descend to the battlefield. He was skilled in archery and also served as a scribe for Imam Hussein, as he was proficient in the Arabic language and recitation of the Quran. He killed a large number of enemies, but when his wounds became severe, he fell to the ground. Imam Hussein hurried towards him, dismounted his horse, and wept over him, placing his noble cheek on the cheek of the young Turkish slave. Aslam opened his eyes, smiled, and said, [1] *"Who is like me, when the grandson of the Messenger of Allah places his cheek on mine?"* Then his noble soul departed.

1 «من مثلي وابن بنت رسول الله واضع خده على خدي»؟

John ibn Haei, the Slave[1]

1 جون بن حيي، مولى أبي ذر الغفاري

John was a slave of Abu Dharr who, after him, chose to be a servant of Imam Hussein. He was a blacksmith and fixed swords. When the battle intensified on the day of Ashura, John approached the Imam seeking permission to fight. Hussein said to him, "O' John, you are relieved of my service. You joined us seeking safety, so do not join our hardships."

2 قال جون لأبي عبد الله: «يا ابن رسول الله، أنا في الرخاء ألحس قصاعكم وفي الشدّة أخذلكم، إنّ ريحي لنتن، وإنّ حسبي للئيم، وإنّ لوني أسود، فتنفّس عليّ في الجنّة ليطيب ريحي ويشرف حسبي ويبيضّ لوني، لا والله لا أفارقكم حتّى يختلط هذا الدم الأسود مع دمائكم»

John fell at the feet of Imam Hussein, kissing them and saying[2], "O' son of the Messenger of Allah, in times of ease, I seek blessings from eating your leftovers, yet in times of hardship, I should abandon you? Indeed, my smell is unpleasant, and my color is dark. Breathe upon me the scent of Paradise.. By Allah, I will never leave your side until my black blood is mixed with yours."

The Imam granted him permission, and John emerged to fight the enemies, and fought until he was martyred.

Hussein walked toward him and stood by his lifeless body, supplicating, "O' Allah, illuminate his face, fragrance his smell, gather him with the righteous, and make him known to Muhammad and his family."

Imam Zainul Abidin said, "When Banu Asad came to bury the bodies of the martyrs in Karbala, they found John after ten days, and a fragrance of musk emanated from him."

MEMBERS OF HUSSEIN'S FAMILY

One by one, the companions of Hussein came forward and asked for his blessings and permission to go fight, bidding him farewell.

When the dust settled, all of the companions lied dead on the plains.

When Hussein saw this tragic scene, he began pleading for help[1]: *"Is there no helper to help us? Is there no one to protect the sanctity of the Prophet's women and children?"*

When the women heard his plea, the sound of their wailing and sobbing rose in the camp.

Within the camp of Hussein, only his family members remained, a steadfast group encompassing the sons of the Commander of the Faithful, the sons of Jaafar and Aqeel, the sons of Hassan, and the valiant sons of Hussein himself. United in purpose, they convened to bid each other farewell and reiterate their commitment to sacrifice their lives for their Master.

1 «ألا هل من ناصر ينصرنا، ألا من معين يعينيا، ألا من ذاب يذب عن حرم رسول الله؟»

ALI AL-AKBAR[1]

The first to step forward was Hussein's eldest son, Ali al-Akbar, who possessed the most luminous face and best of manners.[2] When he came to seek his father's permission. The Imam cast upon him a gaze filled with hopelessness, and his eyes brimmed with tears, streaming down his face.[3]

He raised his face towards the sky and said[4], *"O' God! Be witness against these people; for a young man has been forced to face them, bearing the closest resemblance to Your beloved Prophet in his appearance, conduct, and his speech. Whenever our hearts longed for the presence of Your Messenger, we would look at his face!"*

Ali al-Akbar entered the battlefield, saying[5]:

I am Ali, son of Hussein, son of Ali,
By God, no wicked will rule over me.
With my sword I strike, defending my sire,
A loyal warrior, with Hashemite fire.

Despite his relentless thirst and grievous wounds, he fought bravely, slaying dozens of enemy soldiers. After a fierce campaign, his thirst and wounds led him back to his father. He said "Father, the thirst is killing me and the heavy armor overwhelms me. Is there a way to get a sip of water?".

Hussein consoled his son, assuring him that relief was imminent, saying, "it is only a matter

1 علي بن الحسين الأكبر عليه السلام وعلى قتلته اللعنة والهوان

2 وكان من أصبح الناس وجها وأحسنهم خلقا

3 استأذن أباه في القتال، فأذن له، ثم نظر إليه نظرة آيس منه وأرخى عينه وبكى

4 قال الحسين: «اللهم أشهد فقد برز إليهم غلام أشبه الناس خلقا وخلقا ومنطقا برسولك صلى الله عليه وآله وكنا إذا اشتقنا إلى نبيك نظرنا إليه..»

5 أنا علي بن الحسين بن علي
تالله لا يحكم فينا ابن الدعي
أضرب بالسيف أحامي عن أبي
ضرب غلام هاشمي علوي

of time before you meet your grandfather, who will quench your thirst with his eternal cup".[1]

Filled with heightened valor, Ali Akbar surged forward, displaying courage reminiscent of his grandfather, Imam Ali, on the battlefield. The evil Murrah ibn Munqith attacked him and dealt a blow to Ali's head, causing him to fall on his horse. Blood streamed from his blessed head, drenching the face of his loyal steed. Disoriented and unable to see, the horse inadvertently took Ali into the heart of the enemy. Troops converged upon him from all sides, launching a barrage of sword strikes. The ambush is described with these heartrending words[2]; *"They cut him into pieces!"*

Upon dying, Ali al-Akbar cried so his father could hear him, offering him consolation;[3] *"Father, peace be upon you. Here is my grandfather, the Messenger of Allah, who has quenched my thirst with his most generous cup, from which I shall never thirst again. And he says that a cup awaits you as well."*

Zeinab came out of her tent wailing, saying[4], *"O' my brother! O' my nephew!"*

Imam Hussein rushed to him. When he arrived at his son's side, he threw himself unto him.. Pressing his cheeks against Ali Akbar's, he said,[5] *"May Allah kill those that killed you. My beloved son Ali, without you, this world holds no solace. How audacious they are to transgress*

1 رجع علي الأكبر إلى أبيه وقال: «يا أبت العطش قد قتلني وثقل الحديد قد أجهدني فهل إلى شربة من الماء سبيل» فبكى الحسين عليه السلام وقال: «وا غوثاه! يا بني قاتل قليلا فما أسرع ما تلقى جدك محمد صلى الله عليه وآله فيسقيك بكأسه الأوفى شربة لا تظمأ بعدها أبدا»

2 فقطّعوه إربا إربا!

3 «يا أبتاهُ هذا جَدّي رسول الله قد سقاني بكأسه الأوفى شرّبةً لا أظمأ بعدها أبداً، وهو يقول: «العَجَل العَجَل فإنّ لك كأساً مذخورة». ثم فاضت روحه الطاهرة

4 «وا أخاه.. وا ابن أخاه..!»

5 «قتل الله قوما قتلوك.. بنيّ علي، على الدنيا بعدك العفى، ما أجرئهم على الرحمن وعلى انتهاك حرمة الرسول»

upon the sanctity of the Most Merciful and violate the honor of the Messenger."

Hussein sobbed aloud, drawing attention from the enemy who had not seen him cry like that before.

In his state of betrayal and profound helplessness, Hussein's pleas for assistance resonated. When his cries were heard, even the children answered his call.

THE SONS OF LADY ZEINAB

Abdullah ibn Jaafar, the husband of Lady Zeinab and cousin of Imam Hussein, entrusted his two sons with the duty of sacrificing their lives in defense of Hussein. Aun and Mohammad approached their uncle, seeking his permission to join the battle. With unwavering bravery, they fought until they met their martyrdom.[1]

While they have been commoemorated in Zyara al-Nahyah, historical accounts do not mention Lady Zeinab wailing or shedding tears for the loss of her two sons, neither on the day of Ashura nor thereafter. Her grief was solely reserved for her brother and his beloved children.

1 وقد رود ذكرهما في زيارة الناحية المقدسة: «السلام على عون بن عبد الله بن جعفر الطيار في الجنان، حليف الإيمان، ومنازل الأقران، الناصح للرحمن، التالي للمثاني والقرآن، لعن الله قاتله عبد الله بن قطبة النبهاني. السلام على محمد بن عبد الله بن جعفر، الشاهد مكان إبيه، والتالي لأخيه، وواقيه ببدنه، لعن الله قاتله عامر بن نهشل التميمي»

QASSIM, SON OF HASSAN[1]

1 القاسم بن الحسن عليه السلام، رضوان الله عليه

Qassim, the young orphaned son of Imam al-Hassan, merely thirteen years of age, rose to answer his uncle's plea. Imam Hussein refused to give him permission, unwilling to surrender him to the horrors of war. Qassim fell down, kissing his uncle's hands and feet, and beseeched him for permission. The Imam hugged Qassim and wept, until they both fell unconscious. When they awoke, the Imam granted him the blessing he sought.

Hameed ibn Muslim says, "a boy came to fight us whose face gleamed like a fragment of the moon. Clad in a simple shirt and loincloth, he wielded his sword and raced towards the enemy. The boy wore a pair of sandals, with one lace torn."

I asked about who this boy was, and I was told it was Qassim, the son of Hassan.

He fought bravely saying[2];

If you deny me, I am the son of Hassan,

Son of the chosen Prophet, the trusted one.

Hussein among you is like a captive in chains,

May you never taste heavenly rains.

2 إن تنكروني فأنا نجل الحسن
سبط النبي المصطفى والمؤتمن
هذا حسين كالأسير المرتهن
بين أناس لا سقوا صوب المزن

With valor surpassing his tender age, Qassim laid waste to several enemy soldiers. He then stooped to fix the lace of his sandal, Amr ibn Sa'd al-Azdi[3] declared:

3 عمرو بن سعد الأزدي لعنه الله

54

"By God I shall strike him and make his uncle grieve for him!" Hameed ibn Muslim said, "doesn't it suffice you that he is sorrounded by all those men? By God, if he attacked me, I wouldn't touch him." Amr replied, "by God I shall do it!" He then swung his sword, landing a savage blow upon the boy's head. The young warrior plummeted to the ground, his plea resounding, *"Uncle, save me!"* [1]

1   «أغثني يا عماه!»

With the fury of an enraged lion, Hussein charged toward Qassim. He struck his killer on his arm, cutting it off. Amr screamed for help such that the army heard his plea and rushed to his aid. In the chaos, enemy horses trampled over him.[2] When the dust settled, Hussein was seen standing by the head of his fallen nephew, his body writhing in agony upon the sands. Hussein was heard saying[3], "May God cast them out of His mercy, the people who killed you. May your father and your grandfather be their enemies on Judgement Day." He then cried, *"By God, it is painful for your uncle that you would call upon him, but he does not respond to you, or that he would respond, but his response does not benefit you."*

2   فلما تجلت الغبرة إذا بالحسين على رأس الغلام وهو يفحص برجليه

3   «بُعدا لقوم قتلوك، وخصمهم فيك يوم القيامة رسول الله. عز على عمك أن تدعوه فلا يجيبك، أو يجيبك فلا تنفعك إجابته، يوم كثُر واتره وقل ناصره»

Hussein then held Qassim against his chest, his feet dragging along the ground. Filled with sorrow, he carried him to the tents and laid Qassim beside his beloved son Ali and the other valiant martyrs from his noble household.

Hussein addressed his remaining relatives and said, "My cousins, be patient, for you shall never see disgrace after this day".

Just like that, and one by one, the remaining members of Hussein's family asked for his permission, headed to the battlefield, then after a fierce fight, they were martyred.

ABBAS IBN ALI[1]

Witnessing the mounting death toll, Abbas rose to address his brothers; Abdullah, Othman, and Jafar, sons of Ummul Banin[2]:

"May my soul be ransomed for you! Proceed to the defense of your master until you die in his way."

Abbas' brothers stepped forward and fought valiantly, shielding their Imam with every fiber of their being, placing their faces, throats, and chests in the path of danger to defend their Imam.[3] With hearts ablaze and spirits unflinching, they faced death one by one.

Abbas then stepped forward and positioned himself before his brother. He implored the Imam for permission to fight. Hussein couldn't bear to lose Abbas. He cried and said,

"My brother, you are the bearer of my flag. Without you, my army will crumble, and my enemies would revel in their triumph."[4]

Abbas replied, *"My chest feels constricted, and I am weary of this life. I wish to avenge the treachery of these hypocrites."*[5]

Witnessing Abbas' determination to confront the enemy, he said, "If you must, then go forth and seek some water for these children". Abbas mounted his horse. Shouldering the water container, he fearlessly charged forward, cleaving through the enemy lines as he headed towards the river.

1 أبو الفضل العباس بن علي عليهما السلام

2 «تقدموا بنفسي انتم فحاموا عن سيدكم حتى تموتوا دونه»

3 «فتقدموا جميعا فصاروا امام الحسين عليه السّلام يقونه بوجوههم و نحورهم.»

4 «يا أخي! أنت صاحب لوائي، وإذا مضيت تفرق عسكري»

5 «قد ضاق صدري، وسئمت من الحياة، وأريد أن أطلب ثأري من هؤلاء المنافقين»

1 »كان العباس السقاء قمر بني هاشم صاحب لواء الحسين عليه السلام وهو أكبر الاخوان، مضى يطلب الماء فحملوا عليه«

2 لا أرهب الموت إذا الموت رقا
حتى أواري في المصاليت لقي
نفسي لنفس المصطفى الطهر وقا
إني أنا العباس أغدو بالسقا
ولا أخاف الشر يوم الملتقى

Imam al-Baqer states, *"Abbas was renowned as the provider of water and revered as the luminous moon of Bani Hashem. Standing tall as Hussein's trusted standard bearer, he held the esteemed position as the eldest among his brothers. When the desperate quest for water led him to venture forth, he found himself ensnared by a ring of enemy troops"*. Amidst the clash of steel, he recited the epic[2];

I fear not death, as it draws near,

Among the brave, I'll have no fear.

For the Prophet's sake, my soul I give,

I am Abbas, quenching thirst so others may live

Verse by verse, his voice resonated through the chaos, carrying the weight of his father's legends!

Abbas was surrounded on all sides by a force of four thousand troops who sought to impede his mission. Yet he remained undeterred. He hoisted the standard high above his head and fearlessly charged into the midst of the enemy ranks until they scattered in disarray. He managed to reach the river while overwhelmed by scorching thirst.

When Abbas reached the riverbank, his hands dipped into the clear stream. Whispers of fear swept through enemy lines who knew that if he quenches his thirst, it will mark their demise.

To their astonishment, Abbas spilled the water back into the flowing current. Without drinking a single drop, he filled the container and turned away from the river! He was heard saying[1]:

Abbas, you're worthless after Hussein's fall,
Living or dying, makes no difference at all.
Hussein is dying of thirst, his pain extreme,
So how could you drink from the cool stream?

1 يا نفس من بعد الحسين هوني
وبعده لا كنت ان تكوني
هذا حسين وارد المنون
وتشربين بارد المعين

With the container now full, Abbas mounted his horse, and headed back to his camp. Bent on blocking his path, a horde of enemy troops surrounded him from every direction and launched a relentless assault. Some cunningly concealed behind the cover of trees. As Abbas pressed forward, Zaid ibn Raqaa struck him with his sword and cut off his right arm. He cried out[2],

By Allah, if my hand they dare to sever,
I'll defend my faith, ceasing it never.
I protect the Imam, true in conviction,
Son of the Prophet, purity in depiction.

2 والله إن قطعتم يميني إني
أحامي أبدا عن ديني وعن إمام
صادق اليقين نجل النبي الطاهر الأمين

Abbas held on to both the standard and the water container. As he headed back to the camp, Hakeem ibn Tufail hid behind another bush and struck him on his left arm.

Abbas cried out[1],

O' soul, fear not the disbelievers' might,
Rejoice in God's mercy, shining bright.
With the noble Prophet as our guiding light,
They severed my left hand, an act of spite.
O Lord, consign them to the scorching fire,
In righteous revenge, let justice transpire

After Abbas lost both of his arms, he clenched the water skin between his teeth and embarked towards the camp. However, the enemy was determined to impede his path, raining arrows upon him. One arrow found its mark in the container, causing the water to spill, while another pierced his chest, and yet another struck his eye..!

With the container now drained of its precious contents, Abbas didn't know what to do[2]. Deprived of his hands to wield in battle, his eye to see the enemy, and the water for the children, a sense of despair settled upon him. A man from Bani Tamim emerged stealthily from behind Abbas and ruthlessly struck his head with an iron pole.

Abbas fell to the ground.[3] He cried out, "Brother, *come to me!*"[4] He then bid his brother farewell.

1 يا نفس لا تخشي من الكفار
وأبشري برحمة الجبار
مع النبي السيد المختار
قد قطعوا ببغيهم يساري
فأصلهم يا رب حر النار

2 فوقف العباس متحيّرًا..

3 «وانصرع عفيرا على الأرض يخور في دمه»

4 «أدركني يا أخي!»

When the Imam heard his call, he cried out[2], *"O' brother! O' Abbas!"* He then rushed to him like a falcon descending upon its prey, causing the enemy troops to flee left and right. He screamed[3], *"Where do you flee when you have killed my brother!"*

When he reached his brother, he saw his hands had been severed, his forehead broken, and an arrow was planted in his eye[4]. He leaned over his brother, then sat next him crying[5] saying, *"Now my back is broken. Now my enemy has rejoiced. My brother, who will protect the daughters of the Prophet after you?"*

Hussein then went back to the camp alone while wiping his tears with his shirt sleeve. The women rushed to him and asked about their uncle. Zeinab said: "where is our brother Abbas?"

Hussein didn't say a word. He headed towards Abbas' tent, removed its pillar, letting it fall, signaling that Abbas was gone.[6]

Zainab and the women screamed[7], *"we are lost after you!"* Hussein joined them saying, *"We are lost after you!"*[7]

5   فلما سمع الإمام نداءه قال: «وا أخاه! وا عباساه!» ثم أتاه كالصقر إذا انحدر على فريسته، ففرقهم يمينا وشمالا

6   «إلى أين تفرون و قد قتلتم أخي؟»

7   ثم نزل إليه، فرآه مقطوع اليدين، مرضوض الجبين، السهم نابت في العين

8   فوقف عليه منحنيا، وجلس عند رأسه يبكي

9   «وا أخاه! وا عباساه! وا ضيعتنا بعدك»

10 «وا ضيعتنا بعدك»

THE INFANT

As Hussein (peace be upon him) bore witness to the devastating loss of his beloved relatives and loyal companions, he chose to face the enemy himself. He looked around, and surveyed a landscape strewn with lifeless bodies. He called out,[1]

"Is there no one to defend the sanctity of the women of the Messenger of Allah? Is there anyone devoted to Allah, fearing Him in our regard? Is there anyone seeking help from Allah to assist us? Is there anyone offering support, hoping for what Allah possesses in aiding us?"

Upon hearing this, the air resonated with the anguished cries of the women.

Before Imam Hussein said his last farewell, he asked his sister Zainab to bring him his infant Abdullah. When he saw how the child was dying of thirst, Hussein took his child and headed towards the enemy. He pleaded[2], "O' people! You have killed my brothers, my sons, and my supporters. Now, the only soul left in my care is this innocent child who is dying of thirst, yet he has done no wrong to any of you. I beseech you to offer him a sip of water."

The enemy was split. A few voiced their empathy and suggested they feed him. Others echoed their infamous chant[3]; "Let no member of this household survive!"

---

1 «هل من ذاب يذب عن حرم رسول الله؟ هل من موحد يخاف الله فينا، هل من مغيث يرجو الله بإغاثتنا، هل من معين يرجو ما عند الله في إعانتنا؟»

2 «يا قوم قد قتلتم أخي وأولادي وأنصاري وما بقي غير هذا الطفل وهو يتلظى عطشًا من غير ذنب أتاه إليكم فاسقوه شربة من الماء»

3 «اقتلوهم ولا تبقوا لأهل هذا البيت باقية»

Fearing chaos and insurrection among his troops, Omar ibn Sa'd commanded his chief archer Harmala and said, "Put an end to their dispute"[1]. Harmalah knew what he must do. He retrieved a specially crafted three-pronged arrow typically used for hunting wild animals, and placed it firmly on his bow. Taking aim at the infant's neck, he released the arrow, which struck the tender flesh,[2] "slaughtering him from the jugular vein to the jugular vein."

While the father looked on, the infant fluttered for a moment, his blood gushing from his throat, before wilting, and dying in Hussein's arms!

To console the father's anguish, a voice resonated in the heavens[3], *"Leave him, O' Hussein! For he has a nursemaid in paradise."* Hussein then scooped the blood of the infant and threw it toward the sky, uttering words of acceptance and faith[4], *"What makes this bearable is that it's in God's sight"*.

He then said,[5] *"My complaint is to you, O' Lord. Grant me patience with Your decree. O' Helper of the desperate, there is no deity but You. If this pleases you, then take until you are pleased."* Imam Sajjad says, *"not a drop of his blood came back down."*

Hussein then carried the slain child to the camp. He retreated behind a tent, offering prayers for his deceased son, before delicately excavating a small grave using the tip of his sword. With utmost sorrow, he buried the

1 «اقطع نزاع القوم!»

2 فذبحه من الوريد إلى الوريد

3 «دعه يا حسين فان له مرضعا في الجنة»

4 «هوّن ما نزل بي أنه بعين الله»

5 «لك العتبى يارب، صبرا على قضائك، ياغياث المستغيثين، لا معبود سواك. إن كان هذا يرضيك فخذ حتى ترضى»

child, wrapped in his blood-stained garment. Imam al-Hadi commemorates the infant in Zyarat al-Nahyah[1]; *"Peace be upon Abdullah ibn Al-Hussein, the infant child, abandoned and lifeless, drenched in blood, whose blood ascended to the heavens, slaughtered by an arrow on his father's chest. May Allah curse his assailant, Harmalah ibn Kahil Al-Asadi.."*

When Hussein was left alone, his son Zainul Abedeen emerged from his tent. Stricken by illness, he was too weak to wield his sword. Zainab, his aunt, hurried after him, calling out, "My son, return!" With determination, he replied, *"O' Aunt! Let me to fight for the son of God's Messenger."* Hussein beseeched his sister[2], *"Take him back swiftly, lest the earth becomes bereft of the progeny of Mohammad!"*

1 »السلام على عبد الله بن الحسين الطفل الرضيع، المرمي الصريع المتشحط دما، المصعد دمه في السماء، المذبوح بالسهم في حجر أبيه، لعن الله راميه حرملة بن كاهل الأسدي«

2 قال الحسين: »خذيه لئلا تبقى الأرض خالية من نسل آل محمد صلى الله عليه وآله!«

IMAM HUSSEIN

Left without any supporters, Hussein was described as having lost all hope in life.[1]

He looked right and left searching for helpers only to find his companions slain like sacrificial lambs.[2]

Hussein called out to them[3], *"O' heroes of the battlefield, O' knights of warfare! I call unto you, but you do not answer. If you are asleep I beseech you to wake up. These are the women of the prophet, they have been bereaved for your loss, so rise O' noble ones and protect the progeny from the wicked tyrants. Alas death has prevailed over you, or else you would have supported me."* Then, with a voice that breaks the heart, he called his companions one by one; *"O' Habib! O' Zuhair! O' Nafe'a! O' Muslim.."*[4]

When the children and women heard this, they cried and wailed.

The intense crying of the women and children reached a new peak, so the Imam returned to the camp with a broken heart and a bent back. Heavily wounded, Hussein summoned his women to bid them a final farewell. He advised his women to prepare for affliction[5], to be patient, and to surrender to the will of Allah.

His daughter Sukaina said, *"Father! Have you surrendered to death?"* He replied, *"How

1 كان آيساً من الحياة!

2 نظر يميناً وشمالاً، فلم ير إلاّ من صافح التراب جبينه وقطع الحمام أنينه

3 فنادى: «يا أبطال الصفا ويا فرسان الهيجاء ما لي أناديكم فلا تجيبون، وأدعوكم فلا تسمعون، أنيام أنتم أرجوكم تنتبهون»

4 ثم نادى بصوت حزين يقطّع القلوب: «يا حبيب بن مظاهر، ويا زهير بن القين، ويا نافع بن هلال، ويا مسلم بن عوسجة»

5 «يا سكينة، يا فاطمة، يا زينب، يا أم كلثوم، عليكن مني السلام»

does a man not surrender to death when he has no supporters or defenders?" The women wept and Hussein consoled them and urged them to be patient once again.

He then went to see his son Ali [al-Sajjad] who was bed-ridden and was being cared for by his aunt Zeinab.[1]

When Imam al-Sajjad saw his father, he tried to stand up, but couldn't do so as he was too ill. So he said to his aunt, help me rest my back on your chest *"for this is the son of the Prophet who has come"*. Imam Hussein asked him about his health, and he responded by thanking God. Then Ali ibn al-Hussein asked his father, *"what have you done with these hypocrites?"* Hussein replied, *"My son, they have succumbed to the deception of Satan and forgotten God."*

Overcome with grief, al-Sajjad asked about his uncle Abbas, to which Hussein shared the devastating news, *"Your uncle was martyred and his two hands are left severed by the banks of the river Euphrates."* Al-Sajjad wept intensely until he lost consciousness. Upon awakening, he inquired about others, asking, *"Where is my brother Ali [al-Akbar]? Where is Habib ibn Mudhaher, Muslim ibn Awsajah, Zuhair ibn al-Qayn..?"* The Imam responded, *"my son! Know that there are no men left in the camp except me and you. Those you seek have all been martyred, their lifeless bodies lying upon the ground.."*

1 فلمّا نظر علي بن الحسين إلى أبيه أراد أن ينهض فلم يتمكن من شدّة المرض، فقال لعمته: «سنّديني إلى صدرك، فهذا ابن رسول الله قد أقبل»

Amidst his tears, al-Sajjad implored his aunt, *"Hand me a stick and my sword so that I may lean on the stick and defend the son of God's Messenger, for life holds no value without him."* Imam Hussein intervened, preventing his son from rising, and entrusted him with the care of the family. He announced to the women that al-Sajjad would assume the role of Imam after him.

Hussein then said, *"My son! Convey my greetings to my followers and tell them, my father was indeed killed as a stranger, so mourn him, and he was left as a martyr, so weep for him."* [1]

He then gave him the inheritance of Prophets and secret covenants of divine leadership. He informed him that the prophetic books and other belongings were entrusted to Um Salamah. Imam al-Sajjad recounts, *"On the day my father was martyred, he embraced me against his wounded chest, as blood poured forth.*

He said to me, 'My son, hold fast to this supplication that my mother taught me, passed down from God's Messenger, who received it from Jibra'eel. Whenever you find yourself engulfed in sorrow, despair, trials, or facing a grave and challenging matter, recite the following prayer:

'By the right of Yasin and the Noble Quran, and by the right of Taha and the Magnificent Quran, O' You who has the power to fulfill the needs of the

1 »يا ولدي بلّغ شيعتي عني السلام، وقل لهم: إن أبي مات غريباً فاندبوه، ومضى شهيداً فابكوه«

(الدمعة الساكبة، الوحيد البهبهاني)

supplicants, O' You who knows what lies within the conscience, O' You who brings relief to the afflicted, O' You who brings solace to the distressed, O' Merciful to the elderly, O' Provider for the young child, O' One who does not require explanation, send blessings upon Muhammad and his family'… then mention your wish."[1]

The Imam then headed toward the enemy while saying[2]:

I am Hussein, Ali's own son

I'll never kneel, my battle's begun

Defending kin with all my might

Following the Prophet's guiding light

Abdullah ibn Ammar recounts, *"I have never witnessed a man, devastated and sorrowful after witnessing the massacre of his children and companions, who is more steadfast and courageous than Hussein. Despite numerous men launching attacks upon him, he would fearlessly retaliate, causing them to scatter like a flock of sheep fleeing from a ferocious wolf. He would then return to his position. He would repeatedly say*[6], *'There is no power or strength except with Allah'"*.

When Imam Hussein saw their gathering, which resembled a massive torrent, he raised his hands to the heavens and prayed[1]; *"My Lord, You are my haven in every mishap, my hope in every predicament, my refuge and defender in every ordeal.."*

---

1 «بحق يس والقرآن الحكيم، وبحق طه والقرآن العظيم، يا من يقدر على حوائج السائلين، يا من يعلم ما في الضمير، يا منفّسًا عن المكروبين، يا مفرجا عن المغمومين، يا راحم الشيخ الكبير، يا رازق الطفل الصغير، يا من لا يحتاج إلى التفسير، صل على محمد وآل محمد... وتذكر حاجتك»

2 أنا الحسين بن علي
آليتُ أنْ لا أنثني
أحمي عيالات أبي
أمضي على دين النبي

3 فجعل يكثر من قول: «لا حول ولا قوة إلا بالله العلي العظيم»

1 «اللَّهُمَّ أَنْتَ ثِقَتِي فِي كُلِّ كَرْبٍ رَجَائِي فِي كُلِّ شِدَّةٍ؛ وَأَنْتَ لِي فِي كُلِّ أَمْرٍ نَزَلَ بِي ثِقَةٌ وَعُدَّةٌ..»

Hussein challenged the enemy, daring them to face him in battle. Whoever stepped forward and confronted him met their doom by Hussein's sword.

Observing this, Omar ibn Sa'd shouted at his troops, saying[2], *"Woe unto you! Are you aware of who you are fighting against? This is the son of Ali, the slayer of Arab [warriors]! Attack him for he is but one man!"*

2 »الويل لكم أتدرون من تقاتلون , هذا ابن الأنزع البطين , هذا ابن قتال العرب , فاحملوا عليه حملة رجل واحد!«

The entire army charged at him, but he fought with such valor that they scattered and fled from him like a swarm of grasshoppers.

So four thousand archers came forward. They shot at him and prevented him from reaching his women and children.

Hussein shouted; *"Woe unto you, O' followers of the family of Abu Sufyan! If you have no religion and do not fear the resurrection, then be free in this world. And if you are [truly] Arab, then return to your roots."*

Shimr replied, *"O' son of Fatima! What are you saying?"* Hussein, said, *"I am the one fighting you and you are fighting against me. The women, however, are innocent and bear no responsibility. Therefore, keep your forces away from my family as long as I am alive."* In response Shimr commanded his men[1], *"Leave the man's family and focus your attack on him."*

They then launched a treacherous ambush on our oppressed and lonely Imam.

1 قال اللعين: »إليكم عن حرم الرجل، فاقصدوه في نفسه!«

69

Inflicting numerous wounds upon him, they targeted him relentlessly with a barrage of arrows, making him resemble the spikes on a hedgehog!

Imam Hussein said[2], *"O' nation of evil! How wickedly have you treated the progeny of Muhammad! Know that after killing me you will not fear killing anyone else. By God I hope that my Lord will honor me with martyrdom at your hands, and then avenge me in ways you do not perceive."*

Exhausted by his severe injuries and tormented by unbearable thirst, Hussein paused to rest[3]. As he rested on his horse, a savage named Abul Hutoof hurled a rock in his direction, striking his blessed forehead.

The Imam lifted his shirt to wipe away the blood from his face, and in that moment, a three-pronged arrow, that had been dipped in poison, pierced his chest. The Imam cried out[4], *"In the name of Allah, by Allah, and upon the path of the Messenger of Allah."*

With his head raised towards the sky, he beseeched[5], *"O' Allah! You bear witness that they are slaying a man, other than whom there is no other son of a Prophet upon this earth."*

Hussein reached for the arrow's shaft protruding from his back and pulled it out, causing a torrent of blood to gush forth like a downpour from a rooftop gutter. Placing his hand beneath the wound, he gathered some of the blood and splashed it towards the heavens.

2 فقال الحسين: «يا أمة السوء بئسما خلفتم محمدا في عترته، أما إنكم لن تقتلوا بعدي عبدا من عباد الله فتهابوا قتله وأيم الله إني لأرجو أن يكرمني ربي بالشهادة بهوانكم، ثم ينتقم لي منكم من حيث لا تشعرون»

3 وقف ليستريح ساعة وقد ضعف عن القتال..

ساعد الله قلبك يا صاحب الزمان!

4 «بسم الله، وبالله، وعلى ملة رسول الله»

5 رفع رأسه إلى السماء وقال: «إلهي إنك تعلم أنهم يقتلون رجلا ليس على وجه الأرض ابن نبي غيره»

Not a single drop returned to the ground. He then took a handful of blood from his wound, dyed his head and beard with it, and declared[1], *"I shall meet my grandfather, the Messenger of God, adorned with my blood in this manner, and I shall inform him that such and such murdered me."*

At this point, the sheer weakness caused Hussein to fall to the ground from atop his horse. Cries of the angels reached a new peak. For a while, the enemy Hussein alone, then proceeded to encircle him.

As he laid on the sand, a young boy, approximately nine years old, broke free from his aunt's grasp and rushed towards Hussein, declaring, *"By God, I will not leave my uncle!"*[2] He was Abdullah, the son of Hassan. A killer named Bahr ibn Ka'b aimed his sword at Hussein, prompting the young boy to shout, *"Woe unto you, O' son of the wicked woman! Are you killing my uncle?"*[3] The man struck the boy with his sword. Abdullah instinctively raised his arm to shield himself. The sword severed his arm, leaving it hanging by a mere piece of skin. In agony, the boy cried out, *"My uncle!"*

Hussein embraced the wounded boy and comforted him, saying, *"O' my nephew, be patient. God will reunite you with your righteous ancestors."* Standing close by, Harmalah, the archer, callously shot an arrow at the boy, killing him while he was still in his uncle's embrace.

1 ثم وضع يده ثانيا فلما امتلأت لطّخ بها رأسه ولحيته الشريفة وقال: »هكذا والله أكون حتى ألقى جدي رسول الله وأنا مخضوب بدمي وأقول: يا رسول الله قتلني فلان وفلان«

2 »لا والله لا أفارق عمي!«

3 »ويلك يا بن الخبيثة! أتتقل عمي؟«

The enemy then drew closer and surrounded Hussein as he laid on the ground.

Zeinab stood by the entrance of the tent and screamed[1], *"O' Omar ibn Sa'd! Woe unto you! They are killing Aba Abdillah while you watch?"* Omar turned his wicked face away!

She then addressed the enemy troops. *"Woe unto you! Is there no Muslim among you?"*

No one responded to her!

Shimr yelled at his men, saying[2]; *"Why make this man wait? What's holding you back? He's full of wounds and arrows. Attack him at once!"* So they ambushed him from every direction.

Imam al-Sadeq says[3], *"when those people rushed to sever his blessed head, a call resounded from the depths of God's throne, 'O' nation that has strayed and become bewildered after their Prophet.."* The Imam then said, *"Verily by God they weren't and would never be guided until the one who is sent to avenge the blood of Hussein rises up."*

Hilal ibn Nafe' recounts, "I was standing among the army of Omar ibn Sa'd when a man suddenly cried out, 'Commander! I bring good news! Shimr has slain Hussein!' In haste, I moved through the ranks and witnessed Hussein, drenched in blood, in the throes of death. By God! I had never seen a dying man, drenched in blood, who was more radiant than him. The beauty of his face was such that it distracted me from the thought of killing him.

---

1 «أيقتل أبو عبد الله وأنت تنظر إليه؟»

2 قال اللعين: «ما وقوفكم؟ وما تنتظرون بالرجل؟ قد أثخنته الجراح والسهام»

3 نادى مناد من بطنان العرش: «ألا أيتها الأمة المتحيرة الضالة بعد نبيها، لا وفقكم الله لأضحى ولا فطر»، قال: ثم قال أبو عبد الله فلا جرم والله ما وفقوا ولا يوفقون حتى يثور ثائر الحسين عليه السلام»

In that moment, he asked for a sip of water, but I overheard someone proclaim, 'By God, you shall not taste water until you enter the inferno and drink from its searing oil.' Hussein replied[1], '*I shall seek my grandfather and drink the purest water, and I will tell him what you have done to me.*'"

Hussein's words ignited such a fury within them, as if God had never instilled any trace of mercy in their hearts![2]

THE CATASTOPHE

When Imam Hussein weakened, Shimr called out[1], "*May your mothers grieve over you! Fulfill your orders upon him!*" So they attacked him at once. Thousands descended upon the son of the Prophet!

A group attacked with swords. Another launched with their spears. While another approached with rocks[2].

Imam al-Baqer says[3] that his grandfather had over 300 injuries from inflicted by swords, spears, and arrows. Every strike landed on an existing slash!

A dense, dark fog emerged, accompanied by a fierce crimson wind, obscuring everything in its path, such that people thought divine retribution had been sent.[4]

One hit him on his left shoulder!

An archer closed in with his bow and arrow and aimed it at his throat!

1 نادى شمر: احملوا عليه ثكلتكم أمهاتكم! فحملوا عليه من كل جانب

2 فرقة بالسهام، وفرقة بالسيوف، وفرقة بالرماح، وفرقة بالحجارة

3 عن الباقر عليه السلام: «أُصيب الحسين ووجد به ثلاثمائة وبضع وعشرون طعنة برمح وضربة بسيف ورمية بسهم»

4 وارتفعت في السماء في ذلك الوقت غبرة شديدة سوداء مظلمة فيها ريح حمراء لا يرى فيها عين ولا أثر ، حتّى ظنّ القوم أن العذاب قد جاءهم

75

Another man struck him on his right side!

Sinan ibn Anas came with his spear!

Another stabbed him in the neck!

Zainab, the daughter of Ali and Fatima, climbed on a cliff to see her brother. The entire army was converging on the killing pit. Seeing what was about to happen, she put both of her hands on her head and screamed, *"I wish the sky fell unto the earth.. I wish I were dead.."*

While they took turns to injure him, no one was willing to kill him..

Omar Ibn Sa'd ordered the troops[1], *"Woe unto you! Relieve him!"*

So Shimr charged towards him..[2] As the Imam lied on his back, Shimr first kicked him, sat on his chest, then rolled him over on his face and grabbed his blessed beard.

He pulled out his dagger.. While the angels were in commotion, Shimr began doing the unthinkable!

---

1 قال اللعين: «ويلكم اريحوه!»

2 تقله يا شمر بالله دخليه
تشوفه يلوج ما غير النفس بيه
يخايب خل أخويه حسين ساعه
أغمض له و أمد للموت باعه
تشوفه يلوج ما غير النفس بيه
يخايب خل أخويه حسين ساعه
أغمض له وأمد للموت باعه

THE IMMEDIATE AFTERMATH

Imam Al-Sadiq said[1], *"When they did to Imam Hussein what they did, the angels were in commotion and said, 'O' Lord! This is Hussein, Your chosen one, the son of Your chosen one, and the son of Your Prophet's daughter. [how could this be done to him?]' Allah, the exalted, then revealed the shadow of the Qa'im and said, 'Through him, I shall exact Hussein's revenge.'"*

After the martyrdom of the Imam, the enemy began to ransack his belongings. They stole his clothes, despite being torn to pieces. They snatched his armor. They took his shoes.. One man came and saw a ring in his hand. Instead of pulling it out, he used a knife and cut off his finger!

Omar ibn Sa'd then proceeded to carry out the orders of Ibn Zyad, who had sent him a letter at the start of the battle, saying[2], *"See if Hussein and his companions submit to our rule and surrender to you.. And if they refused to do so, kill*

1 الصادق عليه السلام قال: «لما كان من أمر الحسين ما كان، ضجت الملائكة وقالوا: يا ربّنا هذا الحسين صفيّك وابن صفيّك وابن بنت نبيّك. فأقام الله ظل القائم عليه السلام وقال: بهذا أنتقم لهذا.»

2 انظر فإنْ نَزَلَ حُسَيْنٌ وأصحابُهُ عَلَى الحُكْمِ وَاسْتَسْلَموا فَابعَثْ بِهِم إليَّ سِلْمًا، وإن أبَوا فازحَفْ إلَيهِم حَتَّى تَقتُلَهُم وَمُمَثِّلْ بِهِم.. فَإن قُتِلَ حُسَيْنٌ فَأوطِئ الخَيلَ صَدرَهُ وظَهرَهُ

them and mutilate them. When Hussein is killed, get horses to trample over his chest and back."

So Omar ordered his horsemen to trample the bodies with their hooves. Ten horsemen volunteered and ran over the body of Hussein and his companions several times, even as the women and children watched!

The Imam's horse galloped towards him. He drenched his mane with his blood and ran back to the camp of Hussein. When the women saw the horse without a rider, they wailed aloud and beat their faces. The horse began hitting his head on the ground until he died. Imam al-Mahdi describes this scene[1]:

"When the women saw your steed in a state of disgrace, and they observed your saddle crooked upon it, they emerged from their tents, with disheveled hair, slapping their cheeks, revealing the marks of sorrow. They lamented and called out in wailing, stripped of their dignity. They rushed towards [the pit] where you had been murdered.."

Zeinab screamed, saying[2], *"O' my [grandfather] Mohammad..!"*. She then fell unconscious.

The troops then competed against one another in pillaging the tents of the Holy Prophet, the light of the eye of Fatima. They chased after them and pulled their cloaks off of their heads, all while the women and children cried and wailed for being separated from their loved ones. Then they set the tents on fire,

1 «فلما رأين النساء جوادك مخزيا، ونظرن سرجك عليه ملويا، برزن من الخدور، ناشرات الشعور، على الخدود لاطمات الوجوه سافرات، وبالعويل داعيات وبعد العز مذللات، وإلى مصرعك مبادرات»

2 «وا محمدا! وا جدّاه! وا نبيّاه!»

terrorizing the women and children. Without outer garments or shoes, the women and children had no choice but to run for safety in the desert.

The narrator says, *"I swear to God that I will never forget the sight of Zeinab, daughter of Ali, who with a sorrowful cry said, 'O' Mohammad! May the King of Heaven bless you. This is Hussein, exposed in the open, covered in blood, mutilated, oh the calamity! Your daughters as captives, and our complaint is to Allah.. This is Hussein; beheaded from behind, stripped of his turban and cloak.. May my father be ransomed for the one whose camp was pillaged on Monday*[1].

May my father be ransomed for the one whose body was mutilated and exposed. May my father be ransomed for the one who was anxious until his end and was thirsty until his death and whose beard is dripping blood. This is Hussein who is slain by the children of bastards..'"[2]

---

[1] The calamity of Ashura occurred on Friday. So this is a veiled reference to the root of the tragedy; the accursed Saqeefa, in which the right of the family of the Prophet was usurped and eventually led to his progeny being killed one after the other

[2] «وا محمداه ، صلى عليك مليك السماء، هذا حسين بالعراء، مرمل بالدماء، مقطع الأعضاء، وا ثكلاه، وبناتك سبايا، إلى الله المشتكى.. هذا حسين محزوز الرأس من القفا، مسلوب العمامة والردا. بأبي من أضحى عسكره في يوم الإثنين نهبا، بأبي من فسطاطه مقطع العرى، بأبي من لا غائب فيرتجى، ولا جريح فيداوى، بأبي من نفسي له الفداء، بأبي المهموم حتى قضى، بأبي العطشان حتى مضى، بأبي من يقطر شيبه بالدماء»

Sukaina, daughter of Hussein embraced her father's body. A group of thugs came and forcefully pulled her away from him.

She says at that point, I heard my father's voice[1],

My followers! When water you drink,
Remember me then, let my image sink.

If news of a stranger or martyr reaches your ear,
Lament and mourn for me, let your sorrow appear.

I wish you could witness that mournful day,
And how my camp was in complete disarray,

How I pleaded for water for my innocent child,
Yet their hearts were hardened, mercy defiled.

They quenched his thirst with an arrow's spiteful blow,
Denying him the water that could ease his woe.

In place of the life-giving stream, they showed disdain,
And with an act of aggression, inflicted endless pain.

Despite lying on the sands and his head raised on a spike, the legend of Hussein had just begun.

---

1 شيعتي ما إن شربتم عذب ماء
فاذكروني
أو سمعتم بغريب أو شهيد فاندبوني
أنا السبط الذي من غير جرم قتلوني
وبجرد الخيل بعد القتل عمدا سحقوني
ليتكم في يوم عاشورا جميعا تنظروني
كيف استسقي لطفلي فابوا ان يرحموني
وسقوه سهم بغي عوض الماء المعين

Ashura, a tale with no ending known,
Throughout the ages, its echoes have grown.
Across millennia it resonates, never to fade,
A story immortal, its greatness displayed.

Printed in Great Britain
by Amazon